D0842898

MCLAREN 12C

BY CALVIN CRUZ

TORQUE

Are you ready to take it to the extreme?
Torque books thrust you into the action-packed world
of sports, vehicles, mystery, and adventure. These books
may include dirt, smoke, fire, and dangerous stunts.
WARNING: read at your own risk.

This edition first published in 2016 by Bellwether Media, Inc.

No part of this publication may be reproduced in whole or in part without written permission of the publisher.
For information regarding permission, write to Bellwether Media, Inc., Attention: Permissions Department,
5357 Penn Avenue South, Minneapolis, MN 55419.

Library of Congress Cataloging-in-Publication Data

Cruz, Calvin, author.
  McLaren 12C / by Calvin Cruz.
    pages cm -- (Torque: Car crazy)
  Summary: "Engaging images accompany information about the McLaren 12C. The combination
of high-interest subject matter and light text is intended for students in grades 3 through 7"--Provided by
publisher.
  Includes bibliographical references and index.
  Audience: Ages 7-12.
  Audience: Grades 3-7.
  ISBN 978-1-62617-284-5 (hardcover : alk. paper)
  1. McLaren automobiles--Juvenile literature. I. Title.
TL236.15.M35C78 2016
  629.222'2--dc23
                                    2015013056

Printed in the United States of America, North Mankato, MN.

TABLE OF CONTENTS

.... 4

A FAST RIDE 8

THE HISTORY OF MCLAREN 12

MCLAREN 12C 14

TECHNOLOGY AND GEAR 20

TODAY AND THE FUTURE 22

GLOSSARY 23

TO LEARN MORE 24

INDEX ....

A FAST RIDE

A driver walks up to his McLaren 12C. He reaches for the door and runs his hand along the side of the car. A **sensor** feels his fingers and opens the door. The driver slides into the car. He pushes a button and the powerful **V8 engine** roars to life.

The driver pulls onto a road closed to other traffic. He presses on the gas pedal and the powerful car races down the road. The driver easily steers the 12C around several tight turns. Later, the driver pulls off the road. The car quickly comes to a stop.
What a thrilling ride!

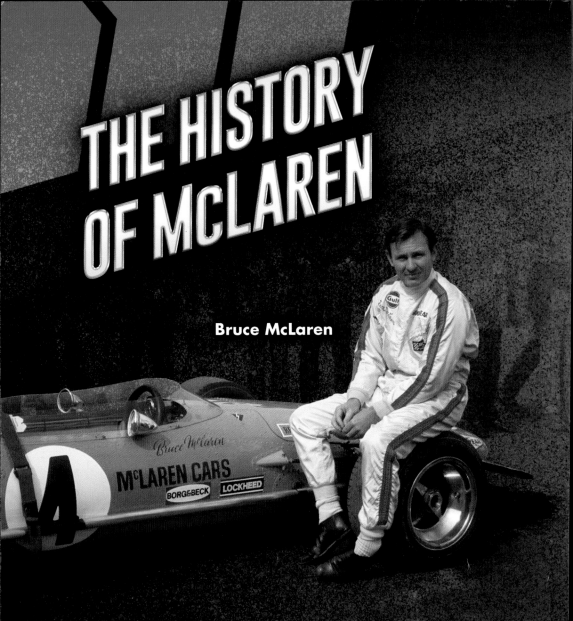

THE HISTORY OF MCLAREN

Bruce McLaren

In the late 1950s, Bruce McLaren was making a name for himself in race car driving. He drove Formula 1 and other race cars. By 1963, he started his own racing team. They built their own race cars.

In the late 1960s, the McLaren team was very successful. They often finished at the top in races. In 1970, Bruce crashed while testing a new car. He passed away, but his team continued racing.

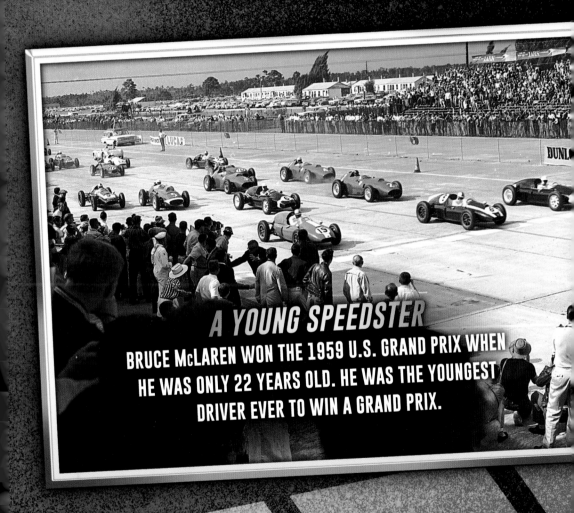

A YOUNG SPEEDSTER
BRUCE McLAREN WON THE 1959 U.S. GRAND PRIX WHEN HE WAS ONLY 22 YEARS OLD. HE WAS THE YOUNGEST DRIVER EVER TO WIN A GRAND PRIX.

The McLaren racing team won many races throughout the 1970s and 1980s. Then they wanted to bring their racing success to the streets. In 1990, McLaren Cars started working on a new **supercar**.

McLaren team at 1974 Canadian Grand Prix

McLaren F1

The McLaren F1 came out to the public in 1993. Its power and design quickly turned heads. Meanwhile, the McLaren team continued to perform well in races.

MCLAREN 12C

The McLaren 12C was first shown off in 2009. It was the company's first supercar since the F1. After 13 years without a supercar on the market, McLaren made the 12C available for purchase in 2011.

Buyers could choose between **coupe** and **spider** versions. Both have two seats, but the spider's roof can be lowered in nice weather.

coupe

RAISE THE ROOF
THE 12C SPIDER'S ROOF CAN BE RAISED OR LOWERED IN 17 SECONDS!

spider

TECHNOLOGY AND GEAR

The McLaren 12C is built to be light and **aerodynamic**. Much of the car is made of **carbon fiber**. This weighs less than metal yet keeps the 12C strong.

The 12C's doors open upward. They are smoother and lighter than regular car doors to increase speed.

The 12C is designed to grip the roads at high speeds. The driver can choose between three drive settings. These change the car's **handling** and power in different driving conditions.

BRAKE STEER

THE 12C USES RACING TECHNOLOGY WHILE TURNING. THE INSIDES OF THE REAR WHEELS BRAKE DURING SHARP CORNERS TO MAKE FASTER TURNING POSSIBLE.

airbrake

MP4-12C

If the driver needs to stop quickly, an **airbrake** pops up on the back of the car. This increases the grip of the tires on the road. It also makes the car less aerodynamic.

The **interior** of the 12C has a race car feel. The steering wheel and **paddle shifters** are based on McLaren's Formula 1 cars. The seats are closer to the center of the car to spread weight out evenly.

It is also made for comfort. The interior is covered in leather and carbon fiber. The driver can even control how loud the engine is inside the car!

paddle shifters

2014 McLAREN 12C
SPECIFICATIONS

CAR STYLE	COUPE OR SPIDER
ENGINE	TWIN TURBO 3.8L V8
TOP SPEED	204 MILES (328 KILOMETERS) PER HOUR
0 - 60 TIME	ABOUT 3.2 SECONDS
HORSEPOWER	616 HP (459 KILOWATTS) @ 7500 RPM
DRY WEIGHT	2,945 POUNDS (1,336 KILOGRAMS)
WIDTH	75.1 INCHES (191 CENTIMETERS)
LENGTH	177.5 INCHES (451 CENTIMETERS)
HEIGHT	47.2 INCHES (120 CENTIMETERS)
WHEEL SIZE	19 INCHES (48 CENTIMETERS) FRONT
	20 INCHES (51 CENTIMETERS) BACK
COST	STARTS AT $239,400

TODAY AND THE FUTURE

The McLaren 12C has been a fan favorite since it was first shown. However, McLaren stopped making the 12C in 2014. They replaced it with a supercar called the 650S. The new car will improve on the 12C's design to keep McLaren at the front of the pack!

McLaren 650S

BUTTERFLY DOORS

SIDE VENTS

AIRBRAKE

SPEED ON SCREEN
THE 12C APPEARED IN THE 2015 MOVIE *FAST & FURIOUS 7.*

GLOSSARY

aerodynamic—having a shape that can move through air quickly

airbrake—a wing on the back of the car that is raised when the driver brakes

carbon fiber—a strong, lightweight material made from woven pieces of carbon

coupe—a car with a hard roof and two doors

handling—how a car performs around turns

interior—the inside of a car

paddle shifters—paddles on the steering wheel of a car that allow a driver to change gears

sensor—a device that feels a driver's hand and opens the door

spider—a car with a roof that can be raised or lowered

supercar—an expensive and high-performing sports car

V8 engine—an engine with 8 cylinders arranged in the shape of a "V"

TO LEARN MORE

AT THE LIBRARY

Georgiou, Tyrone. *Formula 1*. New York, N.Y.: Gareth Stevens Pub., 2011.

Gifford, Clive. *Car Crazy*. New York, N.Y.: DK Publishing, 2012.

MacArthur, Collin. *Inside a Formula 1 Car*. New York, N.Y.: Cavendish Square Publishing, 2015.

ON THE WEB

Learning more about the McLaren 12C is as easy as 1, 2, 3.

1. Go to www.factsurfer.com.

2. Enter "McLaren 12C" into the search box.

3. Click the "Surf" button and you will see a list of related web sites.

With factsurfer.com, finding more information is just a click away.

INDEX

aerodynamic, 14, 17

airbrake, 17, 21

body, 12, 13

brake, 16

Canadian Grand Prix, 10

design, 11, 16, 20

door, 4, 14, 21

drive settings, 16

engine, 4, 18

Fast & Furious 7, 21

Formula 1 race cars, 8, 18

handling, 16

history, 8, 9, 10, 11, 12, 20

how to spot, 21

interior, 18

McLaren 650S, 20

McLaren, Bruce, 8, 9

McLaren Cars (McLaren Automotive), 10, 12, 18, 20

McLaren F1, 11, 12

models, 11, 12, 20

paddle shifters, 18

racing, 8, 9, 10, 11, 16

specifications, 19

speed, 14, 16

U.S. Grand Prix, 9

weight, 14, 18

The images in this book are reproduced through the courtesy of: GuoZhongHua, front cover; McLaren, pp. 4-5, 6-7, 10-11, 12-13, 14-15, 16-17, 18-19, 20-21; Hulton-Deutsch Collection/ Corbis, p. 8; RacingOne/ Getty Images, p. 9; Phipps/ Sutton Images/ Corbis, p. 10 (bottom).